A CALENDAR of FESTIVALS

Barefoot Books
124 Walcot Street
Bath BA1 5BG

First published in Great Britain in 1998 by Barefoot Books Ltd
This paperback edition published in 2005

This book is printed on 100% acid-free paper

Graphic Design by Jennie Hoare, Bradford on Avon
Colour separation by Grafiscan, Italy
Printed in China

Paperback ISBN 1-84148-020-7

British Cataloguing-in-Publication Data: a catalogue record for this book is available
from the British Library

7 9 8 6

A CALENDAR of FESTIVALS

Celebrations from around the World

Retold by Cherry Gilchrist

Illustrated by Helen Cann

Barefoot Books
Celebrating Art and Story

Contents

Contents

Introduction

Festivals are times to celebrate. Wherever you live, there are festivals that you can enjoy. Being at a festival is rather like taking part in a story. At Christmas, if you help to make a crib, or act in a Nativity play, you become part of the Christmas story. The birth of Jesus seems like something that is happening now, not just long ago. And because most festivals are repeated each year, every year we have a chance to remember the story and act it out again.

All societies, going back to ancient times, have had festivals for special times of year – the beginning of spring, for instance, or the first day of the New Year. We mark the rhythm of our calendar with festivals and often there are special customs which are created to 'help' the seasons along, to make the corn grow or the apples ripen. These customs are called rituals, and they are a kind of magical drama. People may light fires to drive evil spirits away, or drink toasts to bring good luck.

Every religion has its festivals too. These often celebrate some important event in the life of the gods or teachers of that religion. You can find stories about Krishna, Buddha, and Jesus in this book. These festivals bring the religious stories alive, and remind us of the important truths that we often forget when we are busy with our everyday lives. They often took over older festivals, so that many of them are very rich in texture, rather like a cake with several layers! The Christian Easter festival, for instance, was set at the time of the ancient spring festival, and Easter eggs represent the new life of spring.

Festivals are joyful occasions – a time to leave our worries behind and celebrate with our neighbours or friends. Festivals are feasts for everyone to share. Many have special food or meals, but they are also feasts in different ways – perhaps a feast of colour, if bright costumes are worn, a feast of music, or drama, or even a feast of wild behaviour! Quite a few festivals encourage people to do things that are not normally allowed, like lighting big bonfires, staying up all night or making a lot of noise! Traditionally, festivals were also a time to show off. There were often competitions and games, beauty parades, archery contests, and a chance to show how well you could sing a song, tell a story, bake a cake or weave a garland of flowers.

In our modern world, where we usually live in small family groups, it's especially important to share our festivals and celebrate together. I hope these stories will help you to enjoy your own festivals, and learn about new ones too!

Cherry Gilchrist

Purim

Jewish
March

Purim is a Jewish festival that is celebrated every year in March, at the time of the full moon in Pisces. The story of Purim goes back a long way in history, perhaps to about 500 BC, to the time after the Babylonians had conquered the Jewish people and driven them out of Jerusalem. It tells how Esther, a young Jewish girl, was made queen of the Persian Empire and bravely saved her people from destruction.

Purim is rather like a carnival. Everyone is allowed to dress up and make jokes. When the Book of Esther is read in the synagogue, people hiss when they hear the name of the villain, Haman, and cheer for the heroine, Esther. In the past, funny plays were also performed, like a kind of pantomime, and children would go round the streets singing and asking for money. Today there are processions and parties, and plenty of feasting – special triangular sweet pastries, known as 'Haman's pockets', are baked and filled with poppy seeds or dried fruit. Presents are exchanged, and money and food given to the poor.

Nobody knows for sure whether the story of Esther really happened, but in any case on the Feast of Purim the Jewish people still remember how they have been threatened during their history, and they joyfully celebrate their escape. The Book of Esther is also an Old Testament book in the Christian Bible.

The Story of Esther

King Ahasuerus of Persia ruled over a great empire that stretched from Africa to India. When he had been king for three years, he decided to celebrate. First he set out a great display of all his treasure for all the officials of his empire to admire. Then he gave a splendid banquet for everybody in the city of Susa – rich and poor alike.

For seven days there was much feasting and drinking, and the king joined in as merrily as anyone. By the seventh day, however, King Ahasuerus had had a little too much to drink. He decided that all his important visitors should also admire his beautiful queen and sent his servants to fetch her. Queen Vashti was giving her own banquet in the women's part of the palace and she refused to come. Why should she be put on show for a lot of strangers to stare at? The king was furious and asked his counsellors what to do next. They advised him to punish her.

'You must send Vashti away. Otherwise all the women in the empire will start disobeying their husbands! Show them what happens to a woman who behaves like this!'

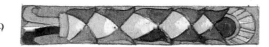

The king took their advice and sent Vashti away. He then decided to find himself a new queen and despatched messengers to all parts of his kingdom to bring back the most beautiful girls to his palace. There they were given baths with scented oils and special beauty treatments for a whole year until they were ready to be sent to the king so that he could choose one of them.

Among them was a lovely young Jewish girl called Esther, who quickly became a favourite at the palace. She had no parents of her own, but every day her uncle Mordecai came to ask how she was. Mordecai's family had been brought to Persia as captives, and he looked after Esther as his own daughter. Nobody knew that Esther and Mordecai were Jewish, however, and Mordecai told Esther that they must keep it a secret.

When King Ahasuerus first saw Esther,
he fell in love with her immediately. He put a
crown on her head and made her his new queen.
He was so happy that he held a banquet in her
honour, gave out presents and ordered a
public holiday as a celebration.

Mordecai still came to court,
but nobody knew that he and
Esther were related, or that either
of them were Jews. Then, one day,
he overheard two of the palace
guards plotting to kill the king. He told
Queen Esther immediately; the two men
were quickly seized and the king's reign
continued safely. Nobody rewarded
Mordecai for this, but he did not mind.
He was welcome at court, and Esther was
happy – that was all he cared about.

But now one of the king's officials, Haman, began to get very ambitious. Ahasuerus had given him special authority at court, and he became very conceited. Many of the other officials and people attending the court bowed down when they saw Haman, but Mordecai did not. Haman was very angry about this. Somehow he discovered that Mordecai was a Jew and decided to take his revenge on all the Jewish people living in the Persian Empire.

'Your Majesty,' he said to the king, 'there is a race of people living in your empire who are very dangerous – they obey their own laws and not yours, and so threaten the safety of your kingdom. I think they should be destroyed, and I could do it for you. I will even pay a large sum of silver into your treasury if you will let me do this.'

'Keep your money, but do whatever you think is necessary,' said the king.

So Haman sent out letters to all parts of the empire stating that every Jew must be killed – man, woman or child. After the messengers had hurried away, the king and Haman sat down to drink together cheerfully. But in the city of Susa itself, people were upset and anxious when they heard the news.

Mordecai was in despair. He put on clothes made of sackcloth and walked through the streets crying bitterly. When Esther heard him, she did not understand what had happened and sent one of the king's servants to find out what the trouble was. But even when

she heard the dreadful news, she did not see how she could help. She did not even think she could talk to the king.

'As everyone knows, no one – not even the queen – may talk to the king without permission,' she told Mordecai. 'He has not called me to him for thirty days now. If I enter the inner courtyard, I will be killed at once unless he holds out his golden sceptre to welcome me.'

'But this could be your chance to help your people, Esther,' replied Mordecai. 'Perhaps that's the real reason you were made queen. If you don't try, you will die anyway when it is discovered that you are a Jew.'

So Esther decided to risk her life. She put on her royal robes and bravely entered the inner court of the king's palace. When the king saw her, he stretched out his golden sceptre to welcome her. She was not going to be put to death!

'What do you want, Queen Esther?' asked the king kindly. 'Whatever you ask, I will give you, even if it is half my kingdom.'

'Your Majesty,' said Esther, 'I've come to invite you to a banquet that I have prepared.'

The king took Haman to Esther's banquet to show him what a wonderful queen he had, and when he had drunk some wine, he was even more loving to her.

'Whatever you wish, you shall have, even if it is half my kingdom.'

'If it pleases your Majesty, come again with Haman to a banquet tomorrow and I will tell you my request.'

The king agreed, and Esther began to prepare her second banquet.

In the meantime, Haman went back home and boasted to his wife, Zeresh, and friends how important he was at court.

'Queen Esther herself invited me to her banquet,' he told them all proudly. But he was also furious to have seen Mordecai back at court again, especially as Mordecai still would not bow to him. Haman was now determined to get rid of him.

'Put up a gallows ready to hang him!' suggested his wife, and all his friends agreed.

'Ask the king for permission in the morning, then make sure it's done,' they said. 'Then you can go to the banquet in a really good mood!'

Haman thought that this was an excellent plan and he set up the gallows in readiness.

But, that night, the king could not sleep. To pass the time, he decided to read some of the palace records. When he came across the story of how Mordecai had saved him from the two wicked guards, he asked his courtiers:

'What reward have we given Mordecai for this?'

'None,' they replied.

Just then, the king caught sight of someone moving about in the outer courtyard in the early morning light.

'Who's there?' he asked.

'It is I,' said Haman, who had come to persuade the king to hang Mordecai.

'Haman, what should the king do for a man that he would like to honour?' asked Ahasuerus.

Haman was delighted at this, thinking that the king wished to give him still more honour and power.

'Dress him in royal robes, your Majesty, and lead him through the city on a royal horse so that everyone can see him.'

'What a good idea!' said the king. 'Yes, fetch the robes and the horse at once – for Mordecai. And you yourself can lead him through the city!'

Haman was furious, but he couldn't say anything. He was forced to do as the king ordered, and lead the man he hated in triumph through the streets of Susa.

Later that same day, the king and Haman went to dine with Queen Esther once again. Once again there was plenty of wine to drink, and the king lovingly asked Esther to tell him what she wished for.

'Your Majesty, I ask you to save the lives of my people, the Jews,' she answered boldly. 'The order has been given that we should all be killed.'

'Who has commanded this?' asked the king in great surprise.

'This wicked man here,' said Esther, pointing to Haman.

'What!' exclaimed the king. And he flew into such a terrible rage that he went straight into the garden to calm himself down again.

Terrified by the king's anger, Haman begged Esther for his life, pushing her down on the couch to try and force her to agree.

Just then, the king returned.

'How dare you attack my queen!' he cried out. 'Take this man away and hang him!'

So Haman was taken away and hanged upon the very gallows that he had set up for Mordecai. And from that time on, the Jews were allowed to live on freely in the empire of King Ahasuerus. In gratitude, the king made Mordecai his chief advisor, knowing him now to be Esther's uncle. Mordecai was remembered as a good, wise governor, loved by all the people - not only the Jews whom he had helped to save. And afterwards, the Jews agreed that every year they would hold a festival to recall the time when Mordecai and Queen Esther came to their rescue.

Holi

Hindu
February/March

Imagine being allowed to squirt all your friends with different-coloured paints! That's what happens at the Indian festival of Holi. It's a Hindu spring festival, sacred to the god Krishna, and held at the time of the full moon in late February or early March. Bonfires are lit, and delicious sweets and snacks are prepared. But the special Holi game is the best: people mix up powdered paints with water, then spray and splash each other with the bright colours.

Hindus believe that all people, even the gods, are reborn – or reincarnated – many times. They also believe that the same god can take many different forms and may sometimes be born into a life on earth. So Krishna, god of love, was born to a human family but is really an 'incarnation' of the great god Vishnu. Indeed, in Hindu art Krishna is always depicted with a blue skin to symbolise his infinite, godly wisdom.

Although his mother and father, Devaki and Vasudeva, were of royal blood, Krishna was brought up in a poor village family. His uncle, the wicked King Kamsa, had threatened to kill him, so Vasudeva smuggled him away to a kind woman called Yasoda, who looked after him as her own child.

Krishna was a naughty little boy, but he grew up into a handsome young god. This story is one of many that are told about Krishna's life.

How Krishna Stole the Butter

'Oh, no!' said Yasoda when she saw the little group of village women arriving at her house. She knew that they were coming to complain as usual. 'Now, Krishna, what have you been up to this time?'

'Nothing, Mother,' replied the young god Krishna, his beautiful eyes wide and innocent. He smiled at her sweetly, and in her heart she had forgiven him already, whatever he might have done.

'Nothing?' said the leader of the women. 'Nothing, did you say? Then who let the calves out this morning? They have been running around everywhere!'

'And who,' said another, 'took my pot of food from the kitchen and gave it to the monkeys to eat? I saw one of them sitting with his greedy, dirty hand stuck in my best pot!'

'And who,' said a third, 'came into my house, piled up all my pillows and climbed up on them, so that he could play with my jewellery?'

'But he is only a little boy!' pleaded Yasoda. 'It is just a game for him!'

'Just a game!' echoed Krishna.

19

One of the women smiled back at him. What a handsome boy he was! Who could think his mischief was any more than a game?

But the leader of the little group did not give up so quickly.

'That was all very well, Krishna, when you were a little baby and could only crawl about on your hands and knees. We forgave you everything then, you and your friends. But you are getting to be a big boy now. You must learn to be responsible and not trouble us or your mother in this way.'

Even she was not really angry any more. Nobody could be cross with Krishna for long. And he had no intention of being a serious, well-behaved sort of child. After all, he was a god! He was here to show everyone that the world itself was beautiful and playful. He loved the flowers of spring and the flowing of water in the river, the sound of wind in the leaves, the fragrant smell of dawn. And, besides which, he was very fond of playing tricks. It was such fun!

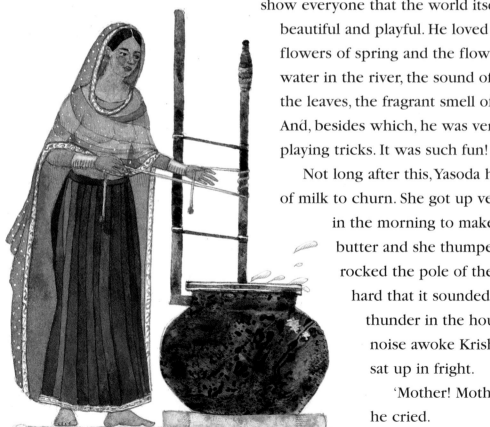

Not long after this, Yasoda had a lot of milk to churn. She got up very early in the morning to make her butter and she thumped and rocked the pole of the churn so hard that it sounded like thunder in the house. The noise awoke Krishna who sat up in fright.

'Mother! Mother!' he cried.

But nobody came. So Krishna got out of bed and came to find Yasoda. When he saw what she was doing, he began to complain.

'Oh, Mother, I called and you didn't come! Haven't you finished your work yet? Where's my breakfast?'

'Now, Krishna,' said Yasoda, hugging him, 'don't worry! I'll give you some bread and curds to eat so that you won't be hungry while I finish my churning.'

She set down a little bowl in front of him. But just then the milk that she was heating in the kitchen began to boil over, and she had to hurry away to save it.

Krishna liked curds, the soft cheesy lumps left over from the butter-making. But he liked butter even better! Some of his friends were playing outside and he called them to come in. They then helped themselves to all the butter that poor Yasoda had spent such a long time making.

And as if that wasn't enough, Krishna broke the big pot with the curds and buttermilk in and snapped Yasoda's churning stick in half! Then, laughing merrily, he and his friends ran outside to eat the butter.

'Come on, you monkeys!' he called. 'Come down from the trees! You can share our feast too!'

When Yasoda found out what he had done, she was furious. Krishna tried to win her over with his most innocent looks, his loveliest smiles and his sweetest kisses, but for once Yasoda ignored him.

'I'll beat you, you naughty little boy!' she cried shrilly.

Krishna started to run away as fast as his little legs could carry him, but Yasoda was quicker and she soon grabbed hold of him.

'Now I've got you!' she said. He looked so frightened that she gave in. 'All right, Krishna, I won't beat you this time!'

Krishna giggled. 'But,' Yasoda went on, 'I'm going to punish you! You're

not going to get away with it! Come with me,' she said sternly, and she took him to the place in the house where the big heavy mortar stood in which she ground all her spices. She decided that if she tied Krishna to it, he could just stay there for a while and not cause any more trouble.

Finding a piece of rope, Yasoda wrapped one end of it around Krishna and tried to tie the other end around the mortar. But it was just a little bit too short. So she found another piece of rope. It was still too short! She tied another, and another, but the rope was never long enough to join Krishna to the mortar. It was another of his tricks – the little god wanted to go free!

At last, when Krishna saw how hot and tired and upset Yasoda was, he took pity on her. He let the rope stretch as far as the mortar and allowed himself to be tied to it.

'Thank goodness!' said Yasoda. 'Now I can get on with my work!'

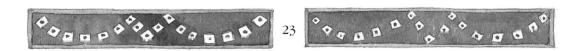

But she did not realise how strong Krishna was. He managed to
crawl right out of the house into the courtyard, dragging the huge,
heavy mortar with him. He crawled as far as the two arjuna trees
which grew there. Then he jerked and rocked the heavy mortar
so hard that it crashed against the trees and uprooted them!

And what was this? They were not ordinary trees after
all, for two men stepped out of the fallen trunks!

They recognised at once who had saved them.

'Thank you, Krishna; thank you, my lord!' they said,
bowing to the young god. 'We were imprisoned in these
trees by the wise teacher Narada. He cursed us because
we were too proud! But we are not proud any more.
Our sin has vanished now!'

They walked respectfully around
Krishna in a circle, bowing to him again.
Then they left on a solemn pilgrimage
to the Himalayan mountains.

The noise of the trees falling was
terrible. Everybody came running.
The cows were so frightened that
they broke their ropes and
stampeded around the village.

Yasoda did not know what to
think. Her naughty little boy had
caused chaos yet again! But she was
relieved that he wasn't hurt, and he
had released these two men from
their prison. Maybe his tricks were
sometimes helpful after all!

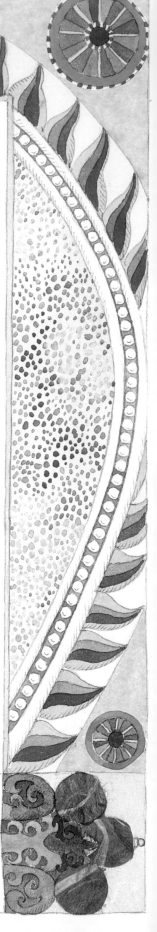
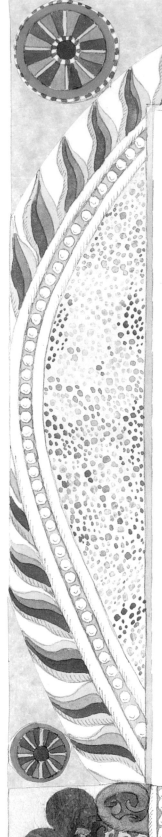

Vesak

Buddhist
May/June

Vesak is a Buddhist festival that is celebrated one day at the time of the full moon in May or early June. The Buddha was born in about 563 BC as an Indian prince known as Siddhartha Gautama. He had rich parents and a comfortable life, but this wasn't enough for him. He wanted to know where we are going in life and how we can rise above the pain and suffering of illness, old age and death. Having discovered the meaning of life beyond the cycle of birth and death, Siddhartha achieved 'enlightenment' and became a Buddha – which is the name for a great teacher who shows other people the way to the truth.

Vesak is the day on which the Buddha became enlightened and began his teaching. People celebrate it by bringing offerings of flowers or fruit to a special meeting place, usually known as the 'shrine hall'. This contains statues of the Buddha and perhaps paintings illustrating his life and teaching. The shrine hall could be in a great temple, or it might simply be a room in someone's house. Monks chant verses from the scriptures, and people will give talks and read aloud, perhaps sharing a meal together afterwards. Buddhists believe that several Buddhas have been born throughout the history of the world and that, when the time is right, a new one will appear to teach us.

Many scriptures and legends recount the life of the Buddha. Some of the details are different, but the main story is the same.

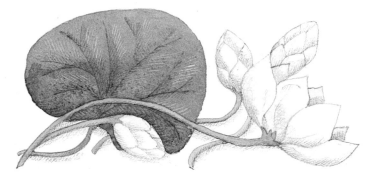

The Life of the Buddha

When the wheel of the universe had turned for a thousand years or so, there was upheaval in the heavens. The gods and guardian angels declared that it was time for a new Buddha to be born and that people on earth were ready to listen to his teachings again.

The mother chosen for this Buddha was Queen Maya, who lived in the city of Kapilavastu in India. Maya had a wonderful dream about her future son. She dreamed that angels carried her off to a house on a silver hill. There they bathed her, laid her on a couch and covered her with heavenly flowers. Then the Buddha himself appeared as a mighty white elephant on a golden hill that lay not far away. Trumpeting loudly, he snatched up a white lotus blossom in his trunk and strode off to find his mother. When he came to Queen Maya's couch, he struck her on the right side with the blossom and entered her body.

When the queen awoke, she told her dream to the king, who summoned sixty-four wise Brahman priests to the palace to ask them what it meant.

'Don't be anxious, your Majesty!' they said. 'If your son leaves the palace and retires from the world, he will become a great spiritual teacher. The message of his teachings will clear away all the clouds of doubt and delusion in the world!'

Four guardian angels watched over the future Buddha while he grew in his mother's womb, to make sure that no harm came to him.

Then, just before her son was born, Maya decided that she would like to visit her relatives in another city, so she set off with her servants, who carried her in a golden chair. On the way, Queen Maya noticed a beautiful grove of trees, filled with birds and flowers, and decided to stop for a while. Alighting there, she knew at once that it was time for her son to be born, and, clasping the strong trunk of one of the trees, she gave birth to her child. The four guardian angels caught him in a golden net as he was born.

All the priests and the wise men examined the baby when he was brought home to the palace. As before, some of them told the king that his

son, Prince Siddhartha, might leave the palace and retire from the world. The king had been too excited before to absorb what they were saying; this time he was not at all happy.

'What will make him retire from the world?' he asked the priests.

'The four signs,' they answered him.

'What are these?'

'An old man, a sick man, a dead man and a monk,' was their reply.

The king was alarmed; he did not want to lose his son. So he decided to keep all old and ill people out of the child's sight. He made sure that the young prince didn't see any dead people or any holy monks. As a result, Siddhartha began to grow up without any idea that we can get sick and old, and that we all must die one day.

At sixteen, Prince Siddhartha was a handsome, merry young man. His life seemed to be perfect. He had three palaces to live in, filled with dancing girls and musicians to entertain him. He was a skilled warrior and, without any formal training at all, he was able to beat all the best archers in Kapilavastu.

Whenever Siddhartha ventured out into the city, the king ordered that all the sick and old people be kept indoors so that his son would not see them. Then one day, when the prince was driving out to the park in his chariot, he noticed an old, grey-haired man crossing the road – the first of the four signs.

'Who's that strange-looking man?' he asked the chariot driver. 'I've never seen anybody like him before!'

The charioteer explained that everybody grows old and their hair turns grey.

Siddhartha returned to the palace, very upset by what he had seen. So the king put more guards around him and tried to distract him with some light-hearted entertainment.

But all the king's efforts were in vain. Siddhartha, when he was next out driving in his chariot, encountered a man who was very ill, and so he learned about sickness. Then, on another occasion, he met a funeral procession and saw the body of a young man being carried away.

'What is the meaning of this?' he cried. 'Why is this young man so still?'

'It is death, my lord,' said the charioteer. 'Death takes us all away from this life. Sometimes it takes us while we are still young.'

Siddhartha was horrified by this. 'Why does this happen? What can we do about it?' he asked himself.

Finally, he encountered a monk – the last of the four signs. As the wise men had predicted, it was this that made Siddhartha decide that he wanted to leave his palace home and seek the meaning of life.

He told his servants to bathe him and dress him for the last time. He asked for his horse to be saddled and, in the middle of the night, he left the palace. But how was he to get out of the city? The king had ordered gates to be made that were so strong and heavy it took a thousand men to open them.

'My horse will jump over them,' thought Siddhartha.

But it was not necessary. At his approach, the gates opened all by themselves, and Siddhartha rode out of the royal city of Kapilavastu.

To mark the beginning of his new life, Siddhartha cut off his long hair and gave away his splendid clothes. He put on the simple robes of a monk and began to beg for his food, as monks do. The first meal was almost impossible to eat – he was used to the delicious food of the palace, and here were everybody's left-overs, all mixed together in the same bowl!

'This is what I wanted,' he told himself sternly. 'When I was in the palace, I longed to be free like the monk that I saw. Now I have this chance, and I must take it.'

For many years, Siddharta tried to live like some of the other holy men,

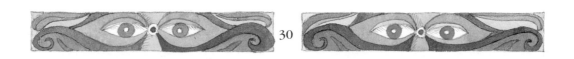

eating hardly any food at all. He lived without proper warmth or shelter until his beautiful golden body grew thin and dark, and he nearly died.

One day, as Siddhartha was sitting under a bodhi tree on the bank of a river, he saw on the opposite bank a fisherman teaching a young boy how to play the lute.

'If you tighten the strings too much,' the fisherman explained, 'they will snap, and if you leave them too slack they won't play, but if they are tuned to the right point, then you will make music.'

Hearing these words, Siddhartha knew at once that to achieve wisdom the strings of one's life should be neither too tight nor too slack; in other words, it is better to be neither too rich nor too poor, neither too hungry nor too well fed.

Sensing that enlightenment was near, Siddhartha began to prepare himself for the struggle that lay ahead. As he sat beneath the bodhi tree, a young woman called Sujata brought him a rich meal of rice and milk, served on a golden dish. She often made

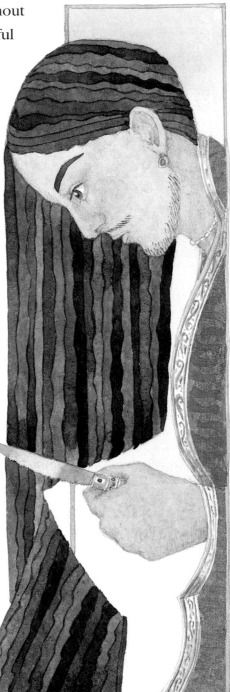

31

offerings at this particular tree, and thought that
Siddhartha must be the god of the tree itself. He
ate the meal gratefully; it was the last food he
would touch for seven weeks. Then, taking the
empty golden dish in his hands, he threw it into
the water.

'If I am to become the Buddha today, let the dish
float away upstream,' he said.

The dish sailed away upstream, where it fell
into the pile of golden dishes that had been
thrown there by the other Buddhas of the past.

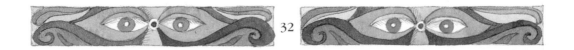

'Another Buddha is on the way!' said the black snake-king from the bottom of the river as he watched the golden dish float by.

Then Siddhartha swore to himself that he would never move from this tree until he had become enlightened.

But the god Mara, who rules all the dreams and delusions of this world, did not want this to happen. So he sent his three beautiful daughters to tempt Siddhartha; but Siddhartha saw that their souls were ugly and could not be moved. Mara tried another tack, inviting Siddhartha to be the king of heaven, but Siddhartha was not interested. Then Mara tried terrifying

Siddhartha with monsters and attacking him with his armies, but Siddhartha saw that all these were mere illusions – and they melted away from him. Showers of hot coals fell as fragrant sandalwood powder at his feet, and swords floated down as flower petals.

Siddhartha sat firm through it all – and at last Mara was defeated. In the heavens, all the gods and angels shouted for joy! The place under the bodhi tree became the Buddha's true throne, the throne of wisdom. For Siddhartha had become enlightened; he now understood the purpose of life – why we are born and why we die.

The Buddha could have returned at once to Nirvana, the special heaven for those who have achieved enlightenment. But he wanted to help others to find the way to enlightenment. So for many years he lived as a teacher, showing people how to practise meditation, how to live a kind and useful life, and how to search for the truth that reveals the meaning of life and death and sets us free.

Tanabata
Japanese
July

Throughout the world, people tell stories about the stars in the sky – why they have particular names and how they got there. In China and Japan, they have a favourite story about two stars which lie on either side of the Milky Way, the broad band of stars that you can see in the night sky. They say that these stars are really two lovers, an oxherd and a weaving maiden, who are separated from each other by the Heavenly River. But once a year, on the seventh day of the seventh month, they are allowed to cross over the river to meet each other.

The Japanese call this day Tanabata, although the festival comes originally from China, and families hold parties to celebrate it. Children decorate bamboo branches in the garden with coloured paper and little bells. As it gets dark, the family gathers there to watch the stars come out and to retell the story of the two lovers. Fireworks are lit and rockets shoot up into the sky to join the Oxherd and the Weaving Maiden, happily reunited for a short spell.

At the Chinese festival, women once used to thread melon seeds together with silver and gold needles, and pray to the two stars for skill in weaving and sewing. Both in China and Japan, the tale of the two lovers is told in many different ways, all based on the original Chinese legend. Here is one version of the story.

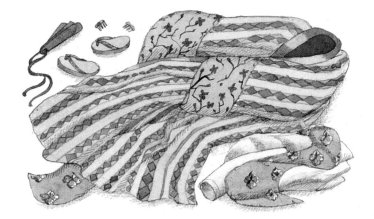

The Oxherd and
the Weaving Maiden

In the highest part of Heaven lived the mighty Jade Emperor. His palace was more magnificent than any of those in which the other gods lived. Here, seated on his jewelled throne and resplendent in his embroidered silken robes, he would command his court. All the other gods had to obey him, and an army of heavenly soldiers was ready to keep them in order if need be. Here also lived Queen Wang, his wife, who gave her famous banquets where the gods were invited to feast on the Peaches of Immortality, grown in the Emperor's own heavenly orchard.

Now, the Jade Emperor had a daughter who used to spin all the silk and weave all the brocade that he needed for his fine robes. Day after day, the Weaving Maiden, as she was known, worked patiently so that the Emperor could always look magnificent in his gleaming silken garments, glistening with embroidered golden dragons. She worked so hard that she never had time to relax. Indeed she began to look so tired that even the Emperor felt sorry for her. He was not a cruel god but he had so much to keep in order that he did not always notice quite as much as he should.

'Take your attendants and go down to earth for a bathe, my dear. Find a nice cool river to swim in, and you will feel much better.'

So the Weaving Maiden floated down to earth with a group of her handmaidens, and straight away they found a lovely river to bathe in. The girls took off their clothes and plunged into the water.

Not far from the river a young man was working in the fields. His father had left him just one ox and a little land to make his living with, and it was hard going. He didn't complain about this, but he felt so terribly alone. He did not even have the time to go courting. But his ox, a clever beast, knew exactly what to suggest:

'Master, leave the ploughing for today and go down to the river. You'll

find a group of lovely girls bathing there. They've left their clothes on the bank. Pick up one set of clothes and hide it, and I promise you that you'll soon have a pretty wife!'

The Oxherd found this hard to believe, but he did what his faithful ox told him and went down to the river. And there, much to his surprise, was a group of beautiful maidens, laughing and splashing each other in the water! And there were their clothes, tossed down in a heap on the bank.

The girls were enjoying themselves so much that they did not notice the Oxherd, and he quickly snatched up one set of clothes and ran off with it. He ran all the way back home, and when he got there, he threw the clothes down an old well in the courtyard.

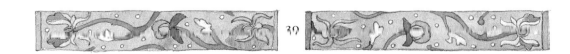

'She'll never find them now!' he thought triumphantly.

Back at the river, the girls decided that it was time to get out and fly back up to Heaven. Chatting merrily to each other, they began to get dressed. All except one – the Weaving Maiden. She could not find her clothes anywhere. What could she do? She couldn't fly back up to Heaven without anything on! In fact, without her clothes, she wouldn't have the power to fly at all. She sat down on the bank and began to cry.

'Don't cry,' came a voice next to her.

Looking up, the Weaving Maiden saw a young man standing in front of her. He had a kind face, and although she was frightened, she knew that he meant her no harm.

'Come with me and be my wife, and I will give you another set of clothes,' he said.

The daughter of the Jade Emperor had no choice. The Oxherd brought her a robe that had once belonged to his mother and it fitted her perfectly. Before long they got married and lived together in his little house. It was not the same as Heaven for the Weaving Maiden, but it was a happy life all the same. She carried on weaving and spinning, and the Oxherd carried on ploughing. With the money that they earned from selling the cloth, they were not too badly off now. And, to tell the truth, the Weaving Maiden was a little sick of all the riches and glory in the Heavenly Palace. It was pleasant to be somewhere where you could

forget all the rules of Heaven and all the huge banquets with important guests. For the time being, at least, she was contented.

Life went on peacefully, and the couple had two children, a son and a daughter. But eventually the Weaving Maiden began to feel homesick. She missed her mother and father, and the Heavenly Palace. She longed to go back for a visit.

Finally she said to her husband,

'Do you remember where you hid my clothes? I've always wondered! We've been married so long that you can surely tell me now?'

'Down the old well in the courtyard,' the Oxherd told her, little suspecting what she planned to do.

The next day, when he was out ploughing, she went to the well and pulled up her clothes from the bottom. Quickly, she brushed off the mud and cleaned them as best she could. Then she put on her robes and in a trice was flying up into the skies and through the gates of Heaven. Up, up she flew, and she didn't stop until she'd arrived back at the doors of the palace of the Jade Emperor.

The Emperor was not pleased, however. Time is different up there, in Heaven, and years can go by on earth which seem only like days or hours in Heaven. Even so, he had noticed her absence.

'Where have you been?' he asked her crossly. 'I have had no one to weave the silk for my robes. Look!' and he showed her the cuff of his robe. 'It's beginning to wear out already.'

The Weaving Maiden took up her heavenly work again, and soon she had almost forgotten her life on earth. But her Oxherd husband missed his wife dreadfully, and the two children were crying for her. He went to his faithful old ox, and threw his arms around the creature's neck, sobbing bitterly.

'Don't cry,' said the ox. 'I have an idea. Put each child in a basket and tie the baskets one on each end of a strong pole. Balance the pole on your shoulders, and then catch hold of my tail. I'll fly you up to Heaven!'

The Oxherd did as he was told. Then the ox flew up into the skies, up to the stars in Heaven, with the Oxherd holding on to his tail for dear life and the children swinging in their little baskets!

At last they arrived at the Heavenly Palace.

'I have come to collect my wife,' the Oxherd said sternly to the guards. 'Let me see His Imperial Majesty the Jade Emperor, and I will explain everything.'

After the Oxherd had told his story, the Emperor called his daughter and asked her if it was true.

'Yes,' she replied, her heart full of love as she saw her husband again.

'Listen,' said the Emperor to the Oxherd, 'my daughter has her work to do here, so I cannot spare her to live with you. But I tell you what I'll do: I'll make you into an Immortal, and you can stay up in Heaven with us. You must live on the other side of the Heavenly River, though, so that you don't distract my daughter from her work. Once a year, however, you can visit each other.'

The Weaving Maiden and the Immortal Oxherd (for so he was now) bowed their heads respectfully and went away to their new homes, one on each side of the mighty rushing golden river of Heaven.

And once a year, all the magpies from earth fly up to Heaven with a twig in their beaks to build a bridge over the river for the two lovers to meet upon.

Halloween
Celtic
October

If you go trick-or-treating on Halloween, did you know that you are taking part in an ancient Celtic festival? The Celtic New Year fell on November 1st and was known as Samhain. The day before was thought to be very dangerous. Ghosts and demons were believed to come up to earth from the underworld, so people lit great bonfires to frighten them away. Eventually the Church turned Samhain into 'All Hallows', a day for the Christian saints, and October 31st became 'All Hallows Eve' or 'Halloween'.

In much of Britain and Ireland, however, Halloween was still thought of as a time of ghosts and witches. It is also a time when people try to guess their future and play games such as bobbing for apples, the sacred fruit of the Celtic underworld.

For the popular 'trick or treat', children knock on doors to ask for a treat and sometimes play a trick if they don't get one! Trick-or-treating is especially popular in America and the term is now widely used in Britain, where it used to be called 'guising'. Groups of children would dress up – 'disguise' themselves – or wear back-to-front shirts, and blacken their faces with soot. Sometimes they sang or told jokes for a penny or two, but sometimes they went round frightening passers-by with their grinning, glowing, turnip lanterns.

The Irish say that the fairies come out to dance on Halloween, and they can be tricky to deal with, as this story shows.

The Halloween Changeling

Once, in the west of Ireland, there lived a young man called Jamie Freel. He was a fine, handsome lad and the kindest son in the world to his widowed mother. Jamie worked long and hard to keep them both in simple comfort in their little house.

'What a great example is young Jamie Freel!' all the neighbours said when their sons wouldn't work so hard. 'Now, why can't you be like him?'

But there came a day when even Jamie felt he needed an adventure. It was Halloween and he decided to go to the big house up the road. The big house was old and deserted, but every year on Halloween the fairies held a party there.

'I'm away to the big house to seek my fortune, Mother!' said young Jamie.

'What? Son, you cannot! The fairies will kill you!'

But Jamie ran out of the door and up the road. At the big house, the windows were all lit up, and the sound of singing and revelry filled the air.

As Jamie pushed the door open, an extraordinary sight met his eyes.

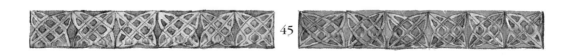

There were hundreds of tiny
people inside – dancing to the music of
flutes, feasting on fairy food and having as
grand a time as you can imagine!

'Welcome, welcome, Jamie Freel!' they cried out. 'Come
and join our revels!'

Jamie joined in with a good heart. He drank and ate, he danced
and sang, he laughed and talked until he clean forgot what time it was
and all the work he had to do the following day!

'Come with us, Jamie Freel!' chorused the fairies at last. 'We're away to
Dublin to steal a fine young lady!'

'I'll come, I'll come!' replied Jamie recklessly.

And with that, they all poured out of the door to where fairy
horses were waiting. No sooner had Jamie climbed upon his
horse than it flew up into the air. Higher and higher, over
the tops of trees and houses it flew, till he could see
everything and everyone down below.

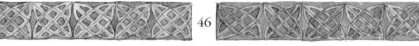

There were all the people eating apples and
roasting nuts for Halloween, but Jamie knew
that he was the only one having a real adventure!
At last they reached Dublin and the fairy troop landed
in a place where the richest families lived and the houses were
very fine. They peered in through a window, and Jamie saw a beautiful
girl asleep in bed with silk and lace covers over her. The fairies flew in,
snatched her up and then dropped a stick on to the bed in her place.

'A stick?' thought Jamie. 'That will fool no one!'

But as he watched, the stick changed shape and became a young girl
just like the one they had carried away!

They began to fly back home, but before they reached the village,
Jamie had quite fallen in love with the young lady. She was the
sweetest, kindest creature he had ever met. Just as he was about to
part with the fairies, quick as a flash he snatched her off her
fairy horse and dropped down with her right outside
his mother's door!

'Jamie Freel, Jamie Freel! Is this the way you treat us?' cried the fairies, and they dropped down too and began to work their wickedest magic.

Before his very eyes, the young lady started to change shape. By turns, she changed into a fierce black dog, a red-hot bar of iron and a weighty sack of wool – but Jamie held fast to her throughout. And at last she came back to her own true self again.

Then one old fairy woman screeched, 'He shan't have her! I'll make her deaf and dumb!' And she threw a cloak over the girl to work the spell.

'Where have you been and who have you brought with you?' cried his mother as they stepped into the house. 'I was afraid that the fairies had made away with you!'

Jamie told his mother all the night's adventures.

'Lord bless us and save us, Jamie!' she exclaimed. 'How is a fine young lady like this to eat cabbage soup with the likes of us?'

The girl was shivering with cold and fear, and Jamie led her to the turf fire to get warm.

'Poor creature!' said Jamie's mother. 'You'll have to work for three of us now, Son!'

'I'll do it,' said Jamie, and he kept his word.

The girl could not hear or speak, and for many days she sat sadly in the cottage, tears trickling down her cheeks as she remembered her father and mother and her fine house in Dublin. But after a while she learned to smile and to feed the pigs and knit socks, so that she kept busy while Jamie made fishing nets and his mother sat spinning in the corner.

And at last Halloween came round again.

'Mother,' said Jamie, putting on his cap, 'I'm off to the old house again to seek my fortune.'

'What!' cried his mother. 'Wasn't once enough for you? Must you take part in devilry and the ruin of innocent souls again?'

'Don't be afraid, Mother,' said Jamie. 'Things will go right, you'll see.'

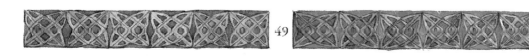

And he made his way to the big house which,
once again, was alive with the sound of music and
singing. But first he stood under the windows a while
and listened to what was being said.

'That was a rotten trick that Jamie Freel played
upon us last year, stealing the fine young lady we went
all the way to Dublin for!' said one fairy.

'Hah! But the laugh is upon him! Little does he
know that three drops from this glass would give her
back her tongue and her hearing!' said another.

Then Jamie went in.

'Here's Jamie Freel – Jamie Freel – Jamie Freel!' the chorus
echoed around the room. 'Come and drink a toast with us from
the Halloween glass!' And they offered him a glass filled with
dark-red liquid.

Jamie snatched it up and ran out of the big house. There was shouting and screeching behind him, and the drink was spilling everywhere, but he didn't stop till he reached his own little house. Panting and gasping, he pushed open the door and made the surprised girl drink the last three drops in the glass.

At once she began to speak, and the first thing she did was to thank Jamie and his mother. They all talked together until the rosy light of dawn came and the fairy lights were extinguished for another year.

The young lady wanted to go back to Dublin to find her father and mother again, so for many days

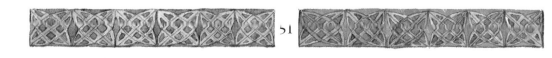

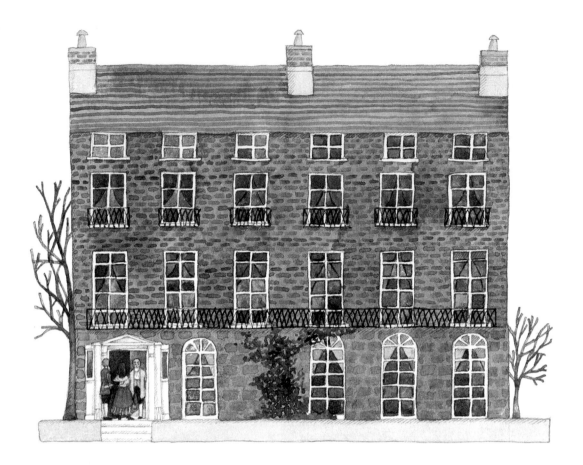

she and Jamie travelled together until they reached the grand house
where she had once lived. They knocked: the door opened, and there
stood her father.

'Father, I've returned!' she announced joyfully. But he just glared at her
and tried to close the door.

'How dare you pretend to be my daughter!' he shouted angrily. 'She is
dead and buried!'

The changeling that the fairies had left was a sickly creature who died
before the year was out.

'Fetch my mother, for she will know me!' said the girl, who was crying
bitterly by now.

Her mother turned pale when she saw the girl standing there.

'Who are you to come in my daughter's place?' she demanded in terror.

'Look, Mother, look at this mark upon my neck!' exclaimed the girl. 'I've had it since I was born.'

'Yes, and so did the daughter that we buried,' answered her mother sharply.

Then Jamie told them the whole story of the fairy changeling. And when her parents at last believed him, they were as joyful as could be.

'We will give you money or jewels for bringing back our daughter,' they said. 'Take whatever you wish!'

'But if Jamie goes, I shall go with him,' said the daughter. 'Do you want to lose me for a second time?'

'Then get married and stay here,' said her father.

'Yes, and your mother is welcome here too!' said the girl's mother.

So Jamie and his young lady were married, and the two families lived together in wealth and happiness for the rest of their lives. And Jamie never forgot how he found his fortune in the strangest of ways with the fairies one Halloween!

Christmas

Christian
December

December 25th is the day on which one of our best-known and best-loved festivals takes place – Christmas Day; for it celebrates the birth of Jesus Christ, the Saviour of the Christian religion. The Bible tells us that he was born in a stable in Bethlehem, when his parents, Joseph and Mary, could find no room to stay anywhere else in the town.

We can't be sure that December 25th was the exact date of Jesus's birthday. Probably priests from the early Christian Church chose this day because it was the time of the midwinter festival, when people celebrated the new light of the sun after the shortest and darkest day of the year.

Some of our Christmas customs come from the Romans. They had a midwinter feast called the Saturnalia at which banquets were held and presents exchanged, and that is how we started to give Christmas presents and enjoy a large Christmas dinner. Other customs are more modern, however. Christmas cards became popular only a hundred years ago or so. And at about the same time, families in Britain began to decorate Christmas trees in their homes, copying their German neighbours. But the tradition of bringing evergreen leaves and branches into the house at midwinter goes back to ancient times.

The Story of the Birth of Jesus

Long ago, in the town of Nazareth, lived a young woman called Mary. She was engaged to a man called Joseph who was a carpenter. All their plans for getting married were going ahead quite smoothly until, one day, an angel appeared to Mary. It was the angel Gabriel, a special messenger from God. He told her that she was going to have a baby.

'Don't be afraid, Mary,' said Gabriel. 'God has chosen you out of all women for this, and he is going to give you a son. You must call him Jesus.'

'How can I have a child?' asked Mary in astonishment. 'I am still unmarried and I haven't been with any man.'

'The Holy Spirit will enter you,' answered Gabriel. 'The power of God will overshadow you. The child himself will be holy, and he will be called the Son of God.'

Mary knelt down before Gabriel and said, 'I am God's servant. I will do his will, whatever it is.'

When she looked again, the angel had disappeared. It was hard to believe that such an extraordinary thing had really happened.

But soon Mary knew that there was a baby in her womb, and it wasn't long before Joseph could see that she was pregnant.

He thought she had been with another man and had been unfaithful to him. He did not see how he could marry her now, so he decided to break off their engagement quietly. But then in a dream an angel came to him, too, and said:

'Joseph, don't be afraid to make Mary your wife. The child she is carrying came from the Holy Spirit. You must call him Jesus, the Saviour, because he will save people from all their sins and from all the wrong that they have done.'

When Joseph woke up, he knew he must obey the angel. He married Mary and they waited patiently for the child to be born.

But before this time, they had to leave Nazareth and travel to another town called Bethlehem. The whole of their country, Israel, was ruled by the Roman emperor Augustus, and now he wanted to count up how many people there were in it. He ordered everyone to go to their own family town and register themselves there. And so Joseph had to go to Bethlehem, the city of David, because his family was descended from King David.

When Joseph and Mary arrived in Bethlehem, the town was crowded with people who had also come to register themselves, and all the inns and places to stay were full. They could not find anywhere to spend the night. Mary felt exhausted and the baby was very heavy inside her now. They looked for shelter everywhere until at last, at one inn, they were allowed to share a stable with the animals. There were no beds or furniture there, nothing except the straw for the animals' bedding and the wooden manger where the beasts ate their food.

During the night, Mary's baby was born. It was a boy – just as the angels had told them. Mary wrapped him round tightly with the special bands of cloth for newborn babies. She had no cradle for her baby, so she laid him down carefully in the manger.

Not far from the town, some shepherds were still sitting up on the hillside. They had to stay awake at night in case any wild beasts threatened their flocks or robbers tried to steal their animals. It was very dark, but suddenly a glorious light began to shine all around them, and in the middle of it appeared an angel. The shepherds were terrified, but then the angel spoke to them:

'Don't be afraid. I have good news for you. Great joy is coming to you and all your people, for today in the city of David a holy Saviour has been born. You can go and find him; you must look for a baby that is wrapped up and lying in a manger.'

And all around them the air was suddenly filled with angels and heavenly spirits making wonderful music as they sang aloud in praise of God:

'Glory to God in the highest heaven. And peace on earth to all men.'

When the angels had disappeared, the shepherds said to each other, 'Come, we must go to Bethlehem straight away and see this for ourselves!'

They hurried down into the town and began to search everywhere. And it was just as the angel had told them – they found the baby Jesus wrapped up and lying in a manger. Mary and Joseph were astonished to hear how the shepherds had come to them, and Mary treasured their story deeply in her heart.

The shepherds worshipped the baby, then went back joyfully to their flocks, praising God for what they had heard and seen.

They were not the only ones to discover the birth of the Saviour. From a far-off country came three Wise Men, who were also looking for the Holy Child. They had learned how to read signs in the skies and how to

see future events written in the stars. When they saw a very special, bright star, they knew that a new Messiah, or Holy King, was about to be born. First they came to Jerusalem, where King Herod lived, the king who ruled the Jewish peoples within the Roman Empire. The Wise Men went around the city, asking everyone they met:

'Where is the child who is born to be King of the Jews? We have seen his star rise in the east, and we have come here to find him.'

King Herod heard what was happening, and he was very upset. He summoned the priests and lawyers of the Jewish people.

'Where will the Messiah be born?'

There were teachings in the scriptures about the coming of the Messiah, the Saviour who would lead the Jews to freedom. The priests and lawyers read out some of these prophecies to him.

'In Bethlehem,' they told him.

Herod knew that the best way to track down this child was to send the three Wise Men to look for him, and so he summoned them.

'Look for the child carefully,' he told them, 'and when you have found him, come and tell me where he is. I shall want to go and pay my respects too.'

But of course Herod did not mean to do any such thing. He simply wanted to stop any other person becoming the King of the Jews.

The Wise Men followed the same star that had brought them on their journey. It moved through the skies and they followed it until it stopped exactly over the place where Jesus lay. Their hearts were full of joy when they found the baby Jesus with Mary and Joseph. They entered the stable and knelt down to worship him. And they gave him precious gifts from their store of treasure – gold, frankincense and myrrh.

But Herod's first plan did not work. The Wise Men did not come back to see him: one of them had a dream warning them not to visit Herod again, so they returned home a different way.

Soon after their visit, an angel again appeared to Joseph in a dream and said, 'Get up, Joseph – you must flee from here at once! Escape to Egypt with Jesus and Mary and stay there till I tell you to return. Herod is going to try and kill the child!'

It was still the middle of the night, but Joseph woke Mary and the family left at once.

Herod soon realised that the Wise Men had tricked him, and he flew into a rage. He ordered his soldiers to kill all the male children under two years old in Bethlehem. For a long time afterwards, the town was full of terrible weeping and wailing as parents grieved for their lost sons.

But Joseph, Mary and baby Jesus got away safely and stayed in Egypt until the angel came to Joseph again in a dream.

'Herod is dead,' the angel told Joseph. 'You may now take Mary and Jesus back to Israel.'

So Joseph took his family back to Nazareth, and it was here that Jesus grew up and began his holy work teaching people how to love God and live in peace together.

Kwanzaa
Caribbean
December

Most of the festivals we know have been celebrated for hundreds or even thousands of years. But here is one that was only started in 1966. Kwanzaa was created by Dr Maulana Karenga to bring black people together and remind them of their African roots. The festival is now very popular with black communities, especially in America.

Kwanzaa begins on December 26th and lasts for seven days. It is held in the home and is a time for families and friends to get together, exchange gifts, sing songs and tell stories. One ear of corn is laid out for each child in the family, and everyone shares a drink from a special Unity Cup, known as Kikombe Cha Umoja.

Seven candles are lit, one for each day of the festival. Each day has a special theme, such as Unity, Faith, Responsibility, or Collective Work, which is remembered in the form of stories and prayers. Everyone is encouraged to use these ideas to strengthen their family life and to help build the community. The stories usually come from Africa or the Caribbean, though any good story can be used.

This tale is for Day Five and is dedicated to Nia, or 'Purpose'. It is about the Warau people, who, the West Indians say, were one of the first groups of people to discover the earth. The story shows that sometimes it's a good idea to follow your own purpose even when other people say that you're mad!

The Warau People Come Down to Earth

Long, long ago, the Warau people lived in a land up above the sky. They were very happy there. Their world was like ours because it had grass and rivers, hills and trees. But one thing was quite different – there were no animals! However, there were all kinds of birds. The Warau people loved birds and most of all they loved their feathers. Why? Well, they liked to make head-dresses out of feathers to wear for dances and feasts. They made the brightest head-dresses you could ever imagine!

Now among the Warau was a handsome young hunter called Okonorote, and he was determined to have the best head-dress of all. Every time he went out with his bow and arrow, he was always looking for the finest birds. And he found plenty, but the feathers were never those special ones that he saw in his dreams.

'Well, those are only dreams!' people said to him. 'Why are you so restless? You don't need anything else. Be happy with what you have!'

But Okonorote didn't listen. He kept on searching until, one day, when he was far away from home, he saw a bird like no other bird he had seen

before. Its feathers were brighter than the sun and more colourful than the rainbow. He wanted it more than anything else in the world.

'Oh, Rainbow Bird! I will never rest until I catch you!'

Okonorote didn't think it would take long. The bird was sitting on a branch and preening its lovely tail feathers of emerald green and ruby red. It almost looked tame – a child could catch it!

Okonorote took aim with his bow. But, in a flash, the bird was gone and only a strange cry floated back towards Okonorote. He was furious!

'I will catch this bird! I swear I will find it or die!'

Okonorote was young and believed he could do anything in the whole wide skyworld. But after five days he was not so sure. Every time he saw the bird, he could never get close enough to shoot it. After five days he was tired – tired of running across the open plains after a flash of brilliant colour, tired of creeping on his belly through the forest, tired of trying to get close to his prey without making the slightest sound.

But then on the fifth day he had some luck. The bird was tired too! It perched on a branch to rest, and shut its eyes. Even a magic rainbow bird can't fly for ever. Okonorote took aim for the hundredth time. He fired. The bird fell heavily to the ground. Okonorote ran to the place where it fell.

But where was it? His rainbow bird was the brightest thing in the forest, but he couldn't see it. He pulled at the branches and prodded in the undergrowth with his bow, but it wasn't there. Was it a spirit bird that had flown back to the gods?

Then he looked down and saw that in front of him was a great hole in the ground. Okonorote got down on his knees and pulled back the grass so he could see it better. He expected it to be some dark pit, with his bird lying at the bottom. But the hole opened out into thin air! And way down below was a new land. Okonorote was looking down on to our earth.

At first it looked rather like home. He could see forests and rolling plains not so different from those he knew already. But what was this?

There were creatures moving around down there, too. There were big flocks of cattle and running herds of deer. There were all kinds of animals, none of which he had ever seen before.

Okonorote knew that somehow he had to get down to this new land. But he needed help to do this, so he went back to tell his people about this marvellous new place. To begin with, nobody would listen to him.

'Foolish boy,' said one of the elders. 'You have had a dream. After five days, of course you were tired. You lay down and slept.'

'Impudent youth,' said another. 'You say this is a new land. But then why haven't we, the wise ones, ever found this hole? Don't boast so recklessly.'

He was nearly ready to give up. Then a few of his friends came to see him, whispering so that the old men wouldn't hear them.

'Okonorote! We believe you! We'll come!'

So they set off together, pretending that they were on just an ordinary hunting trip. Okonorote led them to the right place with no trouble at all.

'Here,' he said. 'Have a look, and you'll see what I mean!'

His friends were so amazed that they could hardly speak! They wanted to get down there as fast as possible. But how could this be done?

'We need a rope,' said Okonorote. 'Better still, a rope ladder.'

The band of young hunters returned home and persuaded the Warau women and girls to weave them a strong rope ladder, as long as they could think of and then half as long again. They pretended it was a new sort of trap for catching birds.

They then took it to the hole, but the ladder wasn't long enough. It didn't even reach the tops of the trees below.

'We need this rope ladder to be a little longer to catch you some good fat birds,' they told the women.

The young men tried again, but the ladder was still too short. It swung in the air above the green grass of the earth.

'What can you be doing?' the women asked them. 'Should we make our fingers sore just because you have crazy ideas that don't work out?'

'Once more – just one more length!' pleaded Okonorote. 'We promise it'll be the last time!'

And it was. The rope just touched the tops of the trees. The hunters cheered.

Okonorote climbed down, feeling giddy and sick as the ladder swung wildly in the sky.

He didn't look down until at last he felt his foot brush against the topmost branch of a tree. Once he touched the ground, he shouted for joy and ran off to explore this new land. He roamed the forests and the grasslands, admiring all the animals that he saw. Large ones, small ones, furry ones, bristly ones, fierce ones, shy ones, spotted ones, striped ones – all were new and wonderful to him. Finally, he shot a deer and roasted it over a fire at sunset. Oh, how good it tasted! Better than anything he had ever eaten before!

When daylight returned, Okonorote climbed back up to the Warau sky country. He ran back home to tell everyone about his adventure.
And when the people heard his story, everybody wanted to go too, even the grumbling old men who hadn't believed him at first.

Not one of the Warau stayed behind. They all climbed down the rope ladder to the earth, with its sparkling rivers, its vast plains and tall mountains, its green forests and craggy rocks. It was all much better than skyland, but best of all were the animals and the fish that they could eat.

Okonorote was still looking for the rainbow bird.

'It must be down here somewhere,' he said to himself.

He never found the rainbow bird, but he found many more wonderful things in his wanderings, like fresh fruit – ripe bananas, sweet guavas and juicy pineapples.

The Warau people loved the earth. They decided to stay here for ever. Only one girl was unhappy. She cried so much that they called her Rainstorm. She tried to go back home, but when she got up to the sky – my goodness, she had got too fat on all that good food! Rainstorm got stuck in the hole in the sky. She struggled and wriggled, but she was wedged tight!

And there she stays till this day, her tears falling now and then as rain. And that's why no one can see through the sky any more, and no one can go back up to skyland. But then, nobody wants to!

New Year
Russian
January

New Year is one of the favourite holidays in Russia. A few days beforehand, people go out into the snowy forest to bring home a fir tree to decorate. Sometimes they choose the tree months ahead and watch it grow till the time is right to cut it. And some people go out to the forest by moonlight to fetch their tree – the snow makes everything so light that you don't even need a torch!

On New Year's Eve itself, many families hold a party where they eat traditional food like pilmeni, or 'hot dumplings', and 'herring in a fur coat' – a kind of beetroot and fish salad. Everybody wears something red for luck, and there are traditional games and songs in honour of the yolka, the fir tree. At midnight glasses are filled with the famous Russian drink, vodka, and everyone drinks a toast to welcome in the New Year: 'S'novim godom!' – 'To the New Year!'

Father Frost is a very important figure in the Russian festival of New Year. In pictures, he sometimes looks like our Father Christmas, and he sometimes brings presents at New Year. But he is really a winter king who rules over the frost and snow that covers Russia all winter long. Father Frost often appears with Snowmaiden, the beautiful daughter of Winter and Spring. There are lots of stories about her, too, and in fact in some versions of this story the girl is known as Snowmaiden – probably because she had to sit in the snow for so long!

Father Frost

Once there was a young girl who lived with her father, her stepmother and her two stepsisters. Her own mother had died when she was little, and her father had married again, but his new wife was bad-tempered and hated the girl. Everything her own two daughters did was perfect, and everything her step-daughter did was wrong. However hard she tried, the girl could not please her.

'Get that girl out of my sight!' shrieked the stepmother one day to her husband. 'I can't stand her any longer! Just take her out to the forest and leave her there!'

'What, in the cold! She'll freeze to death!' he said in alarm.

It was midwinter and deep snow lay all around. Icicles hung from the roofs, the rivers were frozen and even indoors people had to put wood on their stoves night and day to stay warm.

'Yes, why not? She's a good-for-nothing! I won't put up with her any more. Maybe there's somebody out there who'll take a fancy to her and carry her away!'

The girl's father was too afraid of his cruel wife to refuse her. He obeyed her now as he always did, even though he loved his daughter very much. He told himself that maybe his wife was right and some nice young man would find her and marry her, but in his heart of hearts he knew this was a lie. She would die out there in the freezing forest. He harnessed his pony to the sledge and called his daughter.

'Where are we going, Father?' asked the girl as they drove along. She was already cold because her stepmother wouldn't even let her have a rug to wrap herself in.

'Just a little further, my dear,' said her father sadly, as he took her deeper and deeper into the forest.

He set her down by a big tree and told her to sit on a snowy log and wait patiently.

'Someone may come for you, my little one,' he said, as he turned for home. Even his tears turned to ice as he cried for the daughter he thought he would never see again.

The girl sat and waited patiently, but after a few minutes she was bitterly cold. Who was she waiting for? And what should she do if nobody came?

Suddenly, she heard a loud snapping and a crackling. There was something moving above her among the branches of the trees. Crack! Snap! She looked up and saw a great frosty face peering down at her through the branches. It was Father Frost himself!

'How are you, my little maiden?' he asked her in his booming voice.

The girl could not help shivering, but she answered him politely, 'Very well, thank you, Father Frost.'

'Warm enough are you, my dear?' he asked, bending down towards her. The closer he got, the colder she felt, but still she replied, 'Oh yes – yes, thank you, Father Frost. Quite warm, thank you!' But she could scarcely keep her teeth from chattering as she spoke.

As he leaned down further, his breath was like the coldest blast of air that you could ever imagine.

'Oh!' he said, as he saw how she was shivering and chattering and turning blue with the frost. 'No, I think you need something to keep you warm!'

He laid a wonderful heavy velvet cloak around her shoulders, and suddenly she didn't feel cold any longer.

'Thank you, Father Frost,' she said gratefully.
'You are very kind.'

He was pleased with her good manners and, opening
up a chest he had with him, he pulled out a beautiful dress
all sewn with gold and silver thread.

'Here you are, my dear,' he said. 'You will look splendid in this!'

Again the girl thanked him. And now he set down the chest
itself gently at her feet.

'This is for you. May you marry happily and live long! And
remember old Father Frost when you tell your children stories on
your knee!'

Then, with a loud Crick! Crack! Snap! he was off again through
the trees.

The girl could not believe her eyes when she opened the chest.
It was full of gold and silver, of jewels and all kinds of precious
things. And it was hers to keep! But what good would it do her if she
had to stay in the forest for ever?

Meanwhile, the wicked stepmother was cackling to herself as she
prepared the funeral feast.

'That should do it – she's been out there long enough,' she said triumphantly to her husband. 'Now go and fetch her body from the forest!'

The old man harnessed up his pony for the second time and set off with a heavy heart. He did not know which was worse – taking his daughter out to die in the cold, or bringing her body home.

But when he reached the spot far, far into the forest where he had left her, he had the shock of his life. There on the snowy log, dressed in a robe of gold and silver, with a heavy velvet cloak wrapped around her – was his daughter!

And at her feet was a chest of treasure which glittered and sparkled like something straight out of a dream!

He hugged and kissed her. 'I am so glad to see you again, my daughter,' he said.

'Yes,' she answered innocently. 'Someone did come for me, Father, just like you said!'

And so they drove home again together. But was her stepmother pleased to see her arriving dressed like some princess? No, she was not! She shrieked with rage and tossed all the pancakes she had been preparing for the funeral into the stove!

At the same time, she was too crafty to let a good opportunity go by.

'Whatever she has, my daughters must have too! Take them out to the forest! Exactly the same place, mind, and don't you dare get it wrong!' she snarled at her husband.

So before the old man could even take off his boots, she bundled up her daughters, pushed them on to the sledge and ordered her husband back to the driving seat.

He left them in exactly the same place in the forest, and the two girls waited impatiently under the great tree where their stepsister had sat. Before long, they too heard a roaring, cracking, snapping sound in the trees and saw the huge silvery face of Father Frost peering down at them.

'Ho! my beauties!' he said. 'Warm enough, are you?'

One of the sisters stuck out her tongue at him and the other shouted, 'Get out of here, you ugly old man! You're making us colder! Get away, or they won't bring us our treasure!'

'It's treasure you want, is it?' asked Father Frost.

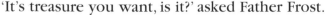

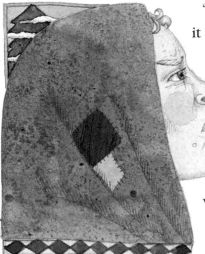

'Yes, our stepsister got some here and we want it too. Twice as much, at least! There's two of us and we both need better husbands than her!'

'Can you see the treasure coming now?' asked Father Frost as he bent closer towards them.

'No, just your horrible whiskers and your nasty old face! Don't you know when you're not wanted? You're freezing us!'

'Yes! Freezing you!' roared Father Frost angrily. 'And so you shall be frozen, you bad-mannered, greedy girls!'

With that, he let loose the coldest frosts in the world and the fiercest winds of the north, and the two girls turned to blocks of ice.

The old man went out once again into the forest to find the girls, and when he returned, his wife ran eagerly to meet the sledge.

'I hope you took care of the jewels on the way home and haven't lost any!' she said. Then she pulled back the blanket and saw the two frozen bodies. She began to scream and cry and tear her hair in rage and disappointment. But she didn't shed one tear for the death of her two daughters.

And suddenly the old man wasn't afraid of her any longer. He took his own daughter far away from that wicked woman, and they lived happily together, just the two of them. They were never afraid or worried any more! There they stayed peacefully, until one day the girl married a kind young man and they all had enough money and treasure to live comfortably for the rest of their lives.

Sources

PURIM
'The Book of Esther', Old Testament

HOLI
Kangra Paintings of the Bhagavata Purana — M. S. Randhawa, National Museum of India, 1960
Hindu Myths — Translated by Wendy O'Flaherty, Penguin, 1975

VESAK
Buddhism in Translation — Henry Clarke Warren, Harvard University Press, 1963
Stories from Dun Huang Buddhist Scripture — Gansu Children's Publishing House (undated)

TANABATA
New Larousse Encyclopaedia of Mythology — Paul Hamlyn, 1959

HALLOWEEN
The Irish Fairy Book — Alfred Perceval Graves, reprinted Senate, 1994
A Treasury of Irish Myth, Legend & Folklore — W. B. Yeats, reprinted Crown Publishers, 1986

CHRISTMAS
'The Gospel according to Matthew' and 'The Gospel according to Luke', New Testament

KWANZAA
West Indian Folk Tales — Philip Sherlock, Oxford University Press, 1966

NEW YEAR
Russian Lacquer Legends Vol. 1 — Lucy Maxym, Siamese Imports Co., 1981
Heroes, Monsters and Other Worlds from Russian Mythology — Elizabeth Warner, Peter Lowe, 1985

GENERAL
Dates and Meanings of Religious & Other Festivals — John Walshe and Shrikala Warrier, Foulsham Educational, 1997
A Dictionary of British Folk Customs — Christina Hole, Hutchinson, 1976
The Dictionary of Festivals — J. C. Cooper, Thorsons, 1990
Festivals Together — Sue Fitzjohn, Minda Weston and Judy Large, Hawthorn Press, 1993

Barefoot Books
Celebrating Art and Story

At Barefoot Books, we celebrate art and story with books that open the hearts and minds of children from all walks of life, inspiring them to read deeper, search further, and explore their own creative gifts. Taking our inspiration from many different cultures, we focus on themes that encourage independence of spirit, enthusiasm for learning, and acceptance of other traditions. Thoughtfully prepared by writers, artists, and storytellers from all over the world, our products combine the best of the present with the best of the past to educate our children as the caretakers of tomorrow.

www.barefootbooks.com